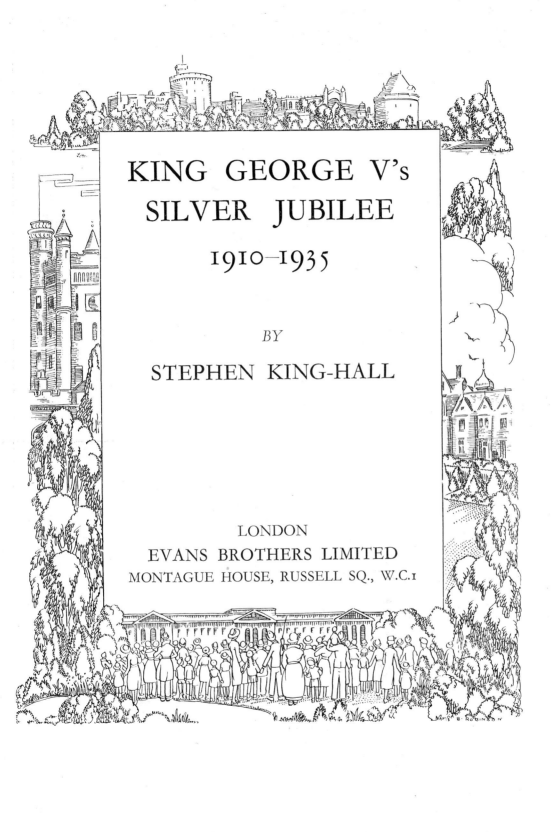

KING GEORGE V's
SILVER JUBILEE

1910–1935

BY

STEPHEN KING-HALL

LONDON
EVANS BROTHERS LIMITED
MONTAGUE HOUSE, RUSSELL SQ., W.C.1

Photo: Vandyk]

HIS MAJESTY KING GEORGE V

HER MAJESTY QUEEN MARY

"*MAY I add very simply and sincerely that if I may be regarded as in some true sense the head of this great and widespread family, sharing its life and sustained by its affection, this will be a full reward for the long and sometimes anxious labours of my reign of well-nigh five-and-twenty years?*"

FROM HIS MAJESTY THE KING'S BROADCAST
MESSAGE TO HIS PEOPLES, CHRISTMAS, 1934

ON the 6th day of May, 1910, His Majesty King Edward VII died at Buckingham Palace in London Town and his son George came to the Throne as George V, King of Great Britain and Ireland and of the British Dominions beyond the Seas, Defender of the Faith, Emperor of India.

That was 25 years ago, and that is why in this year of Our Lord 1935 we celebrate a year of Silver Jubilee.

LONG LIVE THE KING!

LET us celebrate this year of Jubilee by telling the story of these exciting years during which George the Fifth has been our King. Let us flick back the pages of history until we come to that day when our King and Queen rode down to Westminster Abbey in their state coach to be crowned by the Archbishop of Canterbury. The date was June 22nd, 1911.

If you could go backwards in time, and find yourself living in the England of those days, it would seem a strange world, lacking many of the things so necessary to you to-day. For instance, there was no broadcasting, and twelve years were to pass before the B.B.C. came to life. In 1910 wireless had only just come out of the laboratories, and the first commercial wireless messages were being sent across the Atlantic. Motor-cars were still little more than curious luxuries, and in 1910 the women cottagers of Great Britain sent a

letter to the Queen complaining of the hardships brought to them by these newfangled " motors " which raised clouds of dust on the roads, frightened horses, and killed hens. The few people who owned motor-cars were accustomed to have a breakdown every few miles, and as the roads were not tarred, motoring was a dusty business. Men wore goggles, and the ladies special bonnets and veils.

The conquest of the air had just been achieved by 1910, and it was in this year that Paulhan won a prize of £10,000 for the first flight from London to Manchester. Three years later a man called Pégoud startled the world by looping the loop in the air. The last horse-buses were running in London, and taxis were beginning to take the place of hansoms.

Women in Great Britain had no votes, and " Suffragettes " were being sent to prison for the violent measures they took to get the vote for women. Very few women had jobs in business, and generally speaking they were not permitted to do serious work outside their homes. There were few cinemas (they really were "flickers" in those days), and only rich people wore smart clothes. There was a big gap between Society with a big "S" and the Middle Classes, and then another gap between the Middle Classes and the Working Classes.

PERIOD OF GREAT CHANGES

In this year of Jubilee we can look back and see that one of the great changes of the past twenty-five years has been a move towards greater equality between everyone in the nation. It is a movement which is still going on. At the beginning of the reign of George our King, the Liberal party (led by Mr. Asquith) was in power, and working men had just begun to sit in Parliament. Amongst the extreme Liberals or "Radicals" was Mr. Lloyd George, the Chancellor of the Exchequer, who was determined to make a great push forward in what we now call social services (Education, Health and Insurance, Old Age Pensions, etc.). In order to pay for these services he increased taxation, and though nowadays his taxes and his plans would be considered very moderate, in those pre-war years people thought him a very dangerous fellow, almost a revolutionary. However, although there was a terrific struggle between the House of Lords and the House of Commons, Mr. Lloyd George and the Liberals won their way because H.M. the King agreed (on the advice of the Prime Minister, Mr. Asquith) to make 500 new Peers if the House of Lords continued to resist the wishes of the House of Commons.

TROUBLES IN IRELAND

There was an Irish Question. There had been one for years—there still is one to-day (1935). In 1914 His Majesty the King suggested that a conference be held at Buckingham Palace in order to see whether agreement could be reached on the subject of the future government of Ireland.

In these years of 1910–14 the people of Great Britain did not concern themselves very much with foreign news, except that they noticed that across the North Sea the Germans were building a large Navy, and that there was bad feeling between France and Germany. However, in the summer of 1914, just as the families of England were discussing what to do in the holidays, an Austrian Archduke was shot at a place called Sarajevo (June 28th, 1914).

The Austro-Hungarian Government said that the Serbian Government was to blame for the murder, and demanded that Serbia should eat humble pie. The Serbians apologised profusely, but not enough to satisfy the Austrians, who were determined to take advantage of this murder to settle up old scores with the Serbians. The Austrians attacked the Serbians; the Russians backed up the Serbians and the Germans backed up the Austro-Hungarian Government. The French had an alliance with the Russians, and when Germany and Russia went to war with each other, the French were bound to be in the business. The Germans decided that in order to attack France it would be necessary for them to march through Belgium.

OUTBREAK OF GREAT WAR

The Belgians said : "We are not in this row, keep out of our country," but the German armies marched into Belgium. By a treaty signed in 1839 Great Britain had promised to protect the independence of Belgium, and on August 4th, 1914, the British Government warned Germany that if she invaded Belgium we should come into the War. The invasion took place, and at midnight on August 4th, 1914, Great Britain and Germany were at war, and the crowds outside Buckingham Palace were cheering the King and Queen.

On August 4th, 1914, it was cheers, but as the armies went to France and later on to the Dardanelles and Salonika, Palestine and Mesopotamia (now called Iraq), and when news came home of terrible battles which lasted for weeks on end, and the news-

THEIR MAJESTIES IN THEIR CORONATION ROBES

THE CORONATION OF KING GEORGE V

His Majesty was crowned, amid gorgeous pageantry, in Westminster Abbey on June 22nd, 1911.
Here we see the Archbishop of Canterbury about to place the Crown upon His Majesty's head.

papers published column after column of names of men killed fighting on land and sea and in the air, the cheering died down, and people began to understand that the whole nation was bound together in a great and dreadful struggle against the German nation. When a nation is going through a time of hardship and trial the people lift up their eyes for leaders. In Great Britain, Lord Kitchener as a soldier created the new armies which were needed for the War. Mr. Lloyd George succeeded Mr. Asquith as Prime Minister in 1916, and in the darkest days of the War, when German submarines were sinking so many merchant ships that Great Britain was within a few weeks of having to surrender for lack of food, Mr. Lloyd George refused to despair.

But the greatest of all national figures during these War years were Their Majesties the King and Queen. King George visited the armies in France and the Fleet in the North Sea. I remember that after the battle of Jutland he came up to Rosyth and inspected H.M.S. *Southampton*, a light cruiser in which I then had the honour of serving. We had been knocked about a good deal in the battle, and I was lucky enough to have had a narrow escape, since nearly everyone else in my part of the ship was killed or wounded. His Majesty directed me to stand where I had been during the night action, and he noticed that all around me the deck had been torn by shell splinters. He smiled and said : " It does not look as if you were meant to be killed in a battle." I said : " I hope not, Sir ! " He laughed and said, " Well, so do I." His Majesty loved visiting the Fleet, because long before it had seemed likely that he would be King of England he had been a sailor, and a very practical and knowledgeable sailor.

Throughout the War the King visited his fighting forces, and also the factories making munitions of war, in order to give encouragement to his people, and the Queen did her share in an endless round of visits to hospitals where thousands of wounded were lying in suffering and agony. During part of the War two of the King's sons were serving, and running just the

8

same risks as other fighting men. The King and Queen were always anxious to set an example in war work and sacrifice, and when it was felt that the amount of alcoholic liquor being drunk was a waste of money and a hindrance to the war-effort, His Majesty decided that for the duration of the War only teetotal drinks should be used in the Royal Household. The King and his family not only stood for a symbol of unity and war-effort to the people of Great Britain, but they were similarly regarded throughout the Empire.

In August 1914, when Great Britain declared war on Germany, the Dominions and India rallied to the side of the Mother Country. During the War, Australia, Canada, New Zealand and India sent thousands of men to the battlefields, and so won the right to be treated as independent nations at the end of the War.

The War! How can I tell you young people, to whom the Great War is just a piece of history, what those four years of 1914–18 meant to your fathers and mothers? It would be hard enough to do it in a book of 400 pages; it is impossible in a few hundred words. It was terribly costly in life—nearly a million—yes, a million, and that's *ten thousand* hundreds— men were killed in the British armies. The British naval blockade killed off half a million German civilians before their time, and the German fighting forces lost 2 million, killed and missing. Over $1\frac{1}{4}$ million Frenchmen died in battle. The cost in money was fabulous. Some estimates say it cost £40,000,000,000. These are guesses. We know that in 1918 the War was costing the British Government £7 million a day.

Yes—you may say—but what about the War? What happened? Why did it

THEIR MAJESTIES RETURN FROM THE ABBEY

In the famous state coach, drawn by a team of cream ponies, their Majesties return to Buckingham Palace after the Coronation ceremony through enormous crowds of cheering citizens.

A ROYAL FAMILY GROUP

Here we see Queen Victoria, King George's grandmother, with her children and grandchildren, photographed at Osborne House, Isle of Wight. King George, then Duke of York, is standing on the Queen's right.

THE FIRST ROLLS ROYCE MOTOR-CAR

His Majesty, as Prince of Wales, rode in the first Rolls Royce motor-car. By comparing this picture with motor-cars to-day, we see the big changes which have taken place.

THE FIRST AERIAL DERBY, 1912

These machines of the early days of flying form a striking contrast to modern air-liners, many of which are capable of carrying twenty or thirty passengers and of cruising at more than 100 m.p.h.

THE OLD-TIME HORSE-BUSES

Buses drawn by horses were in use in the early days of King George's reign. Although horses are still used on the road to-day, motor transport of all kinds has largely taken their place.

happen? Why did it ever end? It happened, my children, for the same reason that the next War will happen, unless you and all the young people all over the world are extremely careful when you grow up. It happened because men were organised into sovereign states—you must make a special point of discovering what is meant by the word " sovereignty "—and there was no law which the national states were obliged to obey in case of disputes between themselves.

It is waste of time to-day to argue whose fault it was that the War started in 1914 and not in 1909 or 1920. The important point to remember is that, given the kind of international society which existed in 1914, with nations sitting in armed camps growling at each other, a great war was a certainty sooner or later.

STAGES OF THE WAR

From August 1914 to early in 1915 the Germans and the Austro-Hungarians were invading the territories of their enemies, and in the West nearly captured Paris. The Allies were trying to hold up the Central European Powers, whilst they made preparations to invade Germany. By the beginning of 1915 the Allies had succeeded in stopping the advance of the Germans, but were not strong enough to push them back.

Then began the second chapter in the War, during which the British fleet was used to prevent any overseas trade between Germany and the rest of the world, and the armies on each side dug trenches and bombarded each other. The Central European Powers were like a force besieged in a castle. The enemy Powers made several attempts on the East and West to break the ring of armies which was slowly encircling them, and their submarines went to sea and sank Allied merchant ships in order to starve the people of Great Britain, even as the British Navy with its blockade was trying to starve the Germans. During this

THE DELHI DURBAR (1911)

Our King is also Emperor of India, and one of his first tasks after his Coronation was to visit India. Here we see him with the Queen at Delhi, attending the Durbar—a great gathering held in his honour. At the Durbar, the capital of India was transferred from Calcutta to Delhi.

THE KING VISITS THE KAISER (1913)

Our King has earned the title of the "Most Travelled Monarch." As Prince of Wales he travelled extensively in the Empire. This picture shows His Majesty driving in Berlin with the Kaiser. The year after his German visit he went to France to visit the French President in Paris.

second part of the War the Russian revolution took place, and Russia went out of the struggle. At about the same time the United States came into the War on the side of the Allies. Italy joined the Allies in May 1915.

THE ARMISTICE

In July 1918 the Allies were strong enough and the Germans, Austrians, and Hungarians were weak enough to make it possible for the British and French Armies in France to attack the German Armies with success. The Turks—who had joined the German side in 1914—were being beaten in the Middle East, and by November 11th, 1918, there was revolution in Germany and the German Government begged for peace. On November 11th the Armistice was signed, and as soon as this news was announced, thousands of people flocked to Buckingham Palace to cheer the King and Queen. The King replied, " With you I rejoice and thank God for the victories which the Allied Armies have won."

In 1919 a great conference was held at Paris in order to decide what peace terms should be imposed upon the Germans. The Allies squabbled a good deal amongst themselves, but eventually made the Germans agree to very severe terms. The Germans lost all their colonies, were told they would have to pay for the cost of the war (Reparations), were obliged to give up certain areas of territory to France (the Provinces of Alsace-Lorraine) and to Poland and Czecho-Slovakia, two new states created by the Peace Treaties, and were obliged to disband their Army, surrender their Navy and submit to having no air force. The Allies declared that when Germany was disarmed they would do likewise. In another part of the Peace Treaty of Versailles the League of Nations was created. The other defeated Powers (Turkey, Austria-Hungary and Bulgaria) were given equally severe terms.

13

THE MURDER THAT STARTED THE WAR
On June 28th, 1914, the Austrian Archduke Franz Ferdinand was murdered at Sarajevo.   Austria
blamed Serbia for the crime ; Serbia's denial was not accepted, and war became inevitable.

THE PROCLAMATION OF WAR BY GREAT BRITAIN
Great Britain strove to preserve peace, but with the invasion of Belgium by the Germans, she could
no longer remain neutral.   The King's Proclamation of War was read at the Royal Exchange.

THE PRINCE OF WALES IN TRAINING
The Prince joined the Grenadier Guards ; he begged to be allowed to go on Active Service.
His request was granted, and in France he was frequently under fire.

THE KING AT THE FRONT
His Majesty insisted upon visiting the troops in France, and here he is seen in the trenches.

A WOMAN BUS CONDUCTOR

While the War was being waged on so many different fronts, life at home had to go on, and women took the place of men who were at the Front, doing all kinds of jobs normally done by men.

AT WORK ON THE LAND

Before the War, the "Suffragettes" wanted "Votes for Women." The War gave women the chance of showing their ability to serve the nation in thousands of ways. After the War, it seemed natural that women should be given the same political rights as men.

GIVING WARNING OF AN AIR RAID
During the War nearly twelve hundred civilians were killed by air raids in Great Britain.

THEIR MAJESTIES' WAR-TIME RATION CARDS
Food was scarce in war-time, and everybody, including their Majesties, had to have ration cards.

ALL THAT REMAINED OF A FRENCH TOWN

From August 1914 to November 1918 war was waged in Europe, the Near East and on the High Seas. During this period, 7,185,396 men were killed, and 13,500,429 wounded. In addition, whole towns, such as the French town of Louvain shown above, were destroyed by enemy shell fire.

THE KING VISITS HIS FLEET

His Majesty has always been keenly interested in the Navy. Here we see him standing between the guns of H.M.S. Queen Elizabeth on one of his two visits to the Grand Fleet, during the War.

THE KING WELCOMING AMERICAN TROOPS

In 1917 the United States declared War, and in August the first American troops marched through London.

THE PEACE CONFERENCE AT VERSAILLES

In May 1919, the Nations met to decide the terms of Peace, and drew up the Treaty of Versailles.

19

The War was hardly over, and the rejoicings were still taking place in the capital cities of the victorious Powers, when news came to Europe that the Americans had decided not to join the League of Nations which their President had done so much to create. This was bad news for Europe, but it simply meant that France and Great Britain had to set to work to clear up the muddle left over by the War without the

said : "We are all for not letting the Germans off too lightly, but now that the war is over the important thing is to get foreign trade started again, and if Germany is hopelessly and utterly ruined we shall all suffer."

SOME RESULTS OF VERSAILLES

By 1923, the bitter dispute between France and Germany over the fulfilment of the Peace Treaty had reached such a

THE PRINCE IN AUSTRALIA
During the War troops came from all parts of the Empire to help the Mother Country. When the War was over, the Prince toured the Empire, and was received with tremendous enthusiasm.

help of the Americans. A difference of opinion existed between France and Great Britain on the subject of the treatment of Germany. The French said : " It is impossible to trust these Germans, we must use the peace treaty in order to keep them down and out. The Germans are saying they cannot pay for the cost of the War; that is all nonsense. They mean they *won't* pay. We will march into Germany and seize their coal-mines and railways and factories until they do pay." The British

pitch that there was bad feeling between France and Great Britain, whilst France had seized a part of Germany (the Ruhr) in an effort to make her pay the cost of the War. The German money system fell to pieces, and Germany was bankrupt. In 1924, the British Government decided to make an attempt to settle the trouble between France and Germany, and after long discussions it was agreed that Germany should pay a smaller sum than had been first laid upon her.

THE KING OPENS ULSTER'S PARLIAMENT

In 1921 the " Irish Question " was thought to be solved by making Southern Ireland into a Dominion (Irish Free State) and giving Northern Ireland (Ulster) a local parliament.

THEIR MAJESTIES AT WEMBLEY, 1924

The King and Queen showed a keen interest in the products from the Empire displayed at the British Empire Exhibition. Here we see them in the miniature train on " Treasure Island."

21

SIR ALAN COBHAM RETURNS FROM AUSTRALIA, 1926
Here we see Sir Alan Cobham about to alight on the Thames in front of the Houses of Parliament at
the end of his 26,000 miles Australian flight.

THE GENERAL STRIKE, 1926
On May 4th, 1926, a General Strike was called by the Trade Unions in support of the miners who had
been locked out by the mine owners. The life of the country was paralysed for ten days, but, to the
amazement of the world, practically no serious disturbances took place.

At the end of the following year, 1925, an arrangement was made whereby Great Britain and Italy should promise to defend France if France was attacked by Germany, whilst they would defend Germany if she was attacked by France. These were the Locarno Treaties. Soon afterwards (September 1926) Germany was admitted to the League of Nations, and at this time it looked as if at last a real peace would begin. But although the European situation in

world's trading arrangements, and during the period 1919–26, and for some years after this, the British did all they could to persuade other nations to get back to the pre-war state of affairs. But the post-war world considered Great Britain's ideas were out-of-date, and refused to toe the line, and so Great Britain lost much of the business she did before the War, and there were always hundreds of thousands of men and women out of work in the land.

THE KING'S ILLNESS, 1928—29

Following a chill contracted at the Cenotaph on Armistice Day, the King suffered a serious illness. Buckingham Palace was besieged all day by loyal subjects who wished to read the latest bulletins, and in every home families waited anxiously for the nightly wireless news.

1926 looked hopeful, the state of affairs in Great Britain was troublesome.

Ever since the signing of Peace the British had been trying to get back to the conditions which in the pre-war days had made them so prosperous. They had been prosperous because they were great world-traders. In order that trade between countries shall flourish, it is desirable that (a) It shall be as free as possible, that is to say, goods shall not be taxed when they come into a country from abroad, and (b) that the world's international money arrangements (the Gold Standard) shall work smoothly. The War had broken up the

In an effort to make goods cheaply in Great Britain, and so make it easier to sell them abroad, the wages of work-people were reduced, and Great Britain returned to the Gold Standard which she had had to abandon during the War. The hardship of the life of the working class in Great Britain at this time led to serious labour troubles, including a general strike in 1926, which, to the astonishment of foreigners, was settled without serious riots or loss of life.

EVENTS IN UNITED STATES

I mentioned on page 20 that soon after the War the Americans had withdrawn from co-operation in European affairs. The Americans—after the War—were saying: "Let us mind our own business, make a prosperous country over here, and leave these quarrelsome Europeans to stew in their own juices." The Americans found this easier to say than to do, for hardly was the Great War at an end than it began to look as if the next war would take place in the Pacific and the Far East, where Japan was clearly determined to be King of the Castle and build up an Empire on the mainland of Asia at the expense of China. Moreover, the Japanese, British and American Governments were planning to increase the size of their Navies, and it looked as if a competition would start between these three Powers as to which would have the largest Fleet.

THE WASHINGTON CONFERENCE

With these facts in mind, the American Government at the end of 1921 called a conference (the Washington Conference) which produced some treaties, in one of which everyone promised to give China a fair deal, and not take advantage of her weakness and confusion. In another treaty it was agreed that for ten years the British and American Fleets should be of the same size, and the Japanese Fleet was to be three-fifths of this standard size. Apart from the question of peace in the Pacific, there was another reason why the Americans found it difficult to keep out of the business of world affairs. During the War the Americans had lent vast sums of money to the Allies (about £2,000 million), and when the War came to an end the Americans asked to be repaid. The Allies said: "We cannot pay you unless we get the cost of the War from the Germans." The Americans said: "That has nothing to do with the debt you owe us." So much for America for the time being.

EVENTS IN SOVIET RUSSIA

Let us see what had been happening in Russia. In 1917 there was a revolution in Russia and a small number of resolute Communists, led by Lenin, obtained control of the country. They determined to do two things. One, turn Russia into a Socialist state in which the Government would own all "the means of production" and no one would be allowed to own any property except personal property. For instance: a man could own a book or a suit of clothes, but he might not own a factory or a farm. Two, aid and assist revolutionaries in other countries, and so make other nations into Socialist states. These notions seemed extremely shocking to the majority of people in the capitalist states such as Great Britain, France and the U.S.A., and for some years every effort, including war-like operations, was employed in an attempt to upset the Communist or Bolshevist Government in Russia. These attempts failed, and Russia remained Socialist, but, on the other hand, the Russian Communists found that the job of making Russia into a Socialist state was so huge that they really had neither the time nor the energy to worry about world revolution.

The Bolshevists in Russia drew up two five-year plans, which were intended to make Russia a prosperous up-to-date country by the introduction of great quantities of machinery, both in farms and factories. They treated the whole of Russia as if it was one big business owned and managed by the Government. They made a great many mistakes, but learnt by their experiences, and by 1935 it was thought by many people that the Russians had made a fair success of their extraordinary and unusual experiment, but by that time, as we shall see, some of the Russian ideas, which seemed quite impossible to people in capitalist countries in 1923, were being tried out all over the world. The Russians, in fact, decided to do away with private enterprise in a revolutionary and sudden manner, whilst other nations, including our own, were experimenting gradually with schemes by which the Government (on behalf of the whole nation) takes over to a greater or less degree enterprises which in pre-war days would have been run solely for private profit.

*The growth of the interference of the State with private economic life** has taken

* Take the trouble to find out exactly what that sentence means. It is important.—S. K-H.

STALIN (centre), LENIN'S SUCCESSOR AS DICTATOR OF SOVIET RUSSIA

SIGNOR MUSSOLINI (wearing sash): DICTATOR OF FASCIST ITALY

HERR HITLER (bare-headed): DICTATOR OF NAZI GERMANY

place all over the world. Why? Not so much because it is considered to be a good thing, but because this growth of State-control has been found necessary in order to do certain things which most people thought ought to be done, whether they " paid " or not. During the War it was found that the War problems were so huge and difficult that only the Government was big enough to tackle these jobs, and to some extent the same discovery has been made during the peace-time period, especially since about 1929–30, which was the time when the great slump * started.

THE CALM BEFORE THE STORM

As I have already told you, round about 1926 Europe seemed to be settling down into its new frontiers, the Russians were leaving other people alone and being left alone by others ; the League of Nations at Geneva was growing in importance, and there was a general feeling all over the

* Another name for this is the Economic Crisis.

world that things were looking up. It was like one of those sunny days in February or March when the birds begin to sing, the buds begin to open and one says : " Ah ! the dark cold winter is over at last—this is Spring ! " BUT sometimes after such a day there comes a sudden frost, and much damage is done to plants which thought the winter was over. Something like this happened to the world in 1926. For three years, trade seemed to be improving, even Great Britain shared in this sunshine, but by about 1929 there were several signs that the improvement in world affairs was not going to last.

In the first place, much of the improvement was due to the fact that the Americans, who had become very prosperous during the years 1923–27, had been lending money very freely, and not always very wisely, in all parts of the world, and especially to South America and Germany. In fact, Germany had been paying her reparations to the Allies largely with

AMERICA FACES THE WORLD CRISIS

The Economic Crisis affected the United States later than Europe, but when it came the whole Nation looked for a leader. Mr. Roosevelt became President, and his *New Deal* is an attempt to bring back prosperity.

believed by the President to be at the root of American troubles; secondly, to bring about Recovery, and so bring back prosperity to America. In 1935, it was still uncertain whether or not the New Deal would succeed, and the outlook was not very promising.

Nor was trouble confined to Europe and America. In 1931, the Japanese took advantage of the confused state of the world to seize Manchuria, three provinces which belonged to China. The League of Nations—to whom China turned for protection and redress—looked into the matter, told Japan she had done wrong and must give up some of the loot. The Japanese guessed that the League Powers would not have the courage to try and punish Japan if she disobeyed the orders from Geneva. She guessed right, and having turned up her nose at the League,

she gave notice that she would resign therefrom.

LOOKING BACK

Here we must end our account of some of the most important happenings which have marked the first twenty-five years of the reign of King George V. They have been years of tremendous changes; we have been watching the dying off of one kind of world and the birth of a new world. Emperors and Kings whose thrones seemed secure in 1910 have disappeared, frontiers have been changed; new countries have pranced on to the maps. Marvellous new inventions have altered the conditions of our life. Broadcasting, motor-cars, aeroplanes, artificial silk, cinemas, are typical products of these times. In 1910 there were few telephones in Great Britain; in 1935 London was a telephone exchange for the world.

INSIDE BUCKINGHAM PALACE——
The White Drawing Room from the north-west, showing entrance to the Music Room, and the Blue
Drawing Room beyond.

In 1910 the British Empire was ruled from London; by 1935 the Dominions were practically independent and India was travelling fast down the same road. In 1910 Great Britain was a free-trade country and London managed the world's Gold-Standard system; in 1935 Great Britain had tariffs and the British £ was off gold. In 1910 nearly everyone believed that competition in business and trade was " a good thing," and that the less the Government interfered in business the better for all concerned. In 1935 there was hardly a country in the world in which the Government was not engaged in what was called " PLANNING " of industry, commerce and agriculture. In 1910 it was taken for granted that the Parliamentary form of democratic government was the ideal; by 1935 dictatorships in Italy, Germany and Russia, Yugo-Slavia and elsewhere were challenging this view.

What of Great Britain? Emerson wrote : " I find the Englishman to be him of all men who stands firmest in his shoes."

During the troubled times of 1910–35 the British stood firm in their shoes, and when Emperors and Kings were falling like the leaves of the trees in an autumn gale, King George V sat firmly on his Throne.

——THE LONDON HOME OF THEIR MAJESTIES
Another of the beautiful State Rooms at the Palace : the Throne Room, showing the Royal Alcove
and Throne Dais

Why ? For two reasons. In the first place, the Throne, or Crown, as an institution proved itself more than ever necessary to the proper working of a democratic state governed by a Parliamentary system. Moreover, as the British Empire developed, and that part of it represented by the Dominions became more and more independent, men looked around for some link, or bond of Empire, which would take the place of the old controls from London which disappeared when the Dominions joined the League of Nations in 1919 as independent sovereign states. They found this link in " The Crown," for here was something which was above the dust and argument of party politics, and it was something which belonged to all. The King of England was Emperor of India, King of South Africa, Australia, New Zealand and Canada. Even the Irish Free State Government, though desirous in 1935 of leaving the Empire, had said that after this event they were still prepared to give recognition to the King as the head of an Empire with which they hoped to have specially friendly relations.

But institutions are dead things without men, and so we come to the second reason why the Crown is more firmly established in 1935 as part of our constitution than it

31

ROYAL SILVER JUBILEE, 1910—1935

has ever been before. We come to George the MAN. What is he like? He is a sailor-man. He is full of sound common-sense. He can lose his temper, and he loves a good joke. He believes in moving with the times, but *one step at a time*. He loves yacht-racing, is a keen stamp-collector and a great country gentleman. He has devoted his life to the service of his country, and in this heavy task he has been supported and comforted by his gracious consort, Queen Mary. He is a family man, and very fond of playing with his grandchildren. He is the greatest and probably the most hard-working of the Civil Servants of the Empire. He is a keen listener-in to wireless pro-grammes, and one of the best broadcasters.

of the present time. He is a first-class broadcaster for one simple reason, and that is because when he talks to the millions of his people his words come from his heart as well as from his head. Everyone, rich and poor, grand and humble, feels: " This man is talking to me, and he is meaning every word he says. He wrote this broad-cast himself. This is not an official speech." They are right. Our King is also our friend, our companion, our fellow countryman who has rejoiced and who has sorrowed with us during the last twenty-five years. The King sits firmly on his Throne; but his Throne is in reality not in Buckingham Palace or Westminster Abbey, but in millions of British hearts.

On behalf of all the readers of this book, we respectfully wish Your Majesty many more years of prosperity, happiness and service in the welfare of your people.

[*Printed by R. Clay and Sons, Ltd., Bungay, Suffolk.*